Simplified Cooking From The 1930s With Pictures

*The Era Of The Great Depression
Recipes for Tenacity and Grit
Made Easy*

by

LUNAR PUBLISHING

Simplified Cooking From The 1930s With Pictures: The Era Of The Great Depression Recipes for Tenacity and Grit Made Easy

Simplified Cooking From The 1930s With Pictures: The Era Of The Great Depression Recipes for Tenacity and Grit Made Easy

SEE MORE OF MY BOOKS HERE

Simplified Cooking From The 1930s With Pictures: The Era Of The Great Depression Recipes for Tenacity and Grit Made Easy

Table of Content

Cucumber Sandwiches

Stuffed Celery

Fruit Cocktail

Baked Brie

Vegetable Platter with Dip

Rice Pudding

Bread Pudding

JellO

Apple Crisp

The Depression Cake

Ambrosia Salad

Date Nut Bread

Chocolate Mayonnaise Cake

Pineapple UpsideDown Cake

Molasses Cookies

Butterscotch Pudding

Raisin Pie

Shoofly Pie

MAIN DISH

Meatloaf

Chicken à la King

Beef Stroganoff

Chicken Pot Pie

Deviled Ham

Creamed Spinach

Beef and Noodles

Tuna Noodle Casserole

Liver and Onions

Baked Ham with Pineapple

Stuffed Bell Peppers

Creamed Chipped Beef on Toast

Chicken and Dumplings

Pork Chops with Applesauce

Veal Parmesan

Beef Wellington

Oxtail Soup

CONCLUSION

INTRODUCTION

In a quiet corner of an antiquarian bookstore, nestled between weathered volumes of history and faded novels of bygone eras, sat a rather unassuming book: "Simplified Cooking from the 1930s." Its cover, once vibrant and alive with colors that whispered of a different time, now bore the marks of countless hands that had caressed its spine. The pages, worn and tinged with age, held secrets of an era when cooking was an art, a science, and a testament to resourcefulness.

This particular cookbook, however, was no ordinary culinary guide. It was a time capsule, transporting readers to an age when simplicity was not just a trend but a way of life. Opening its pages felt like stepping into a sepia-toned world, where recipes were more than a list of ingredients and instructions; they were a narrative, a story spun around each dish.

Among the yellowed pages adorned with elegant calligraphy and hand-drawn illustrations, there was a short story, a tale woven within the fabric of recipes. It spoke of a young woman named Margaret, a chef with a fervor for the culinary arts. Born in an era marked by economic hardships and a longing for simplicity, she found solace and joy in the kitchen.

Margaret's story was a reflection of an era when resources were scarce, yet creativity abounded. She navigated the challenges of the 1930s with grace, turning modest pantry staples into gastronomic delights that adorned the table. Her tales were accompanied by vivid, hand-drawn pictures, each one depicting a moment in her culinary journey. Whether it was the art of preserving seasonal harvests or conjuring up a hearty meal from meager rations, her ingenuity shone through each image.

As the cookbook opened a window to Margaret's world, the pictures within it not only showcased the steps of a recipe but also painted a vivid

portrait of the zeitgeist. The images were more
than visual aids; they were a glimpse into the
soul of an era marked by resilience, simplicity,
and an unwavering passion for culinary
craftsmanship.

"Margaret's Kitchen Chronicles," as the section
was titled, presented more than just recipes. It
was a narrative of survival, adaptation, and the
joy found in the simplest of life's pleasures. Each
picture was a snapshot of an ethos—an homage
to an era where a pinch of innovation and a dash
of frugality blended to create culinary
masterpieces.

Amidst the stories and illustrations, "Simplified
Cooking from the 1930s" unveiled the essence
of an age when cooking was not merely a means
of sustenance but a celebration of tradition,
innovation, and the art of making do with what
one had at hand.

The pages of the cookbook whispered the secrets
of a time when kitchens were sanctuaries, and

each meal was a labor of love and creativity. Margaret's vivid descriptions, interwoven with the pictures, brought to life the thrifty yet sumptuous dishes that graced dining tables in an era shadowed by economic trials and culinary inventiveness.

The images captured moments like Margaret's beaming face as she presented a frugal but delectable carrot cake, born from the necessity of rationing sugar and eggs, or the joyous depiction of her improvising a comforting vegetable stew from the harvest of a modest backyard garden. The colors and strokes in each drawing vividly portrayed the satisfaction of creating something delightful out of the simplest of ingredients.

In "Margaret's Kitchen Chronicles," the cookbook became more than a repository of recipes; it evolved into a testimony of resilience, resourcefulness, and the unwavering spirit that thrived in times of scarcity. With every turn of a page, readers could almost sense the aroma of the dishes wafting from the pictures, evoking memories of a time when flavor and flair transcended limitations.

However, the real magic lay not just in the culinary concoctions but in the stories behind them. Each picture narrated a saga of adapting, improvising, and transforming humble ingredients into culinary treasures. The book, in essence, was a time machine that transported its readers to an era where the heart of every household lay in the aroma of a well-cooked meal and the gathering around the table to share stories, laughter, and simple yet hearty fare.

As the reader delved deeper into Margaret's world, the resonance of those bygone days was not just about cooking; it was a reflection of a generation's spirit, an embodiment of making the most out of life's offerings, even when they seemed scarce.

The pictures within the cookbook weren't just visual aids but windows into an era when cooking was a symphony of flavors, colors, and emotions—crafted not only from ingredients but from a profound sense of community, resilience, and the unyielding human spirit.

As this unique cookbook promised a journey through history, it also held the potential to inspire a new generation, inviting them to embrace the ethos of resourcefulness, simplicity, and the joy found in the everyday art of cooking—a legacy that transcends time.

The story of "Simplified Cooking from the 1930s" wasn't just about an era; it was a timeless ode to the heart and soul poured into every dish, every image, and every word, inviting readers to savor not just the flavors but the essence of an era that etched its mark on culinary culture.

This cookbook wasn't just a book of recipes; it was a living, breathing testament to a time when cooking was an art, a story, and a journey through history itself.

Simplified Cooking From The 1930s With Pictures: The Era Of The Great Depression Recipes for Tenacity and Grit Made Easy

Simplified Cooking From The 1930s With Pictures: The Era Of The Great Depression Recipes for Tenacity and Grit Made Easy

DRANKS

Gimlet

The Gimlet is a timeless classic that combines
the sharpness of lime with the smoothness of gin
or vodka. It's a simple and refreshing cocktail
that's perfect for any occasion.

Prep Time: 5 minutes Cook Time: 0 minutes
Servings: 1

Calories: 164 Fat: 0g Carbs: 4g Fiber: 0g
Sugar: 4g Protein: 0g

Ingredients:
- 2 oz gin or vodka
- 3/4 oz fresh lime juice
- 1/2 oz simple syrup (or more to taste)
- Lime wheel or twist for garnish

Instructions:
1. Fill a shaker with ice.
2. Add gin or vodka, fresh lime juice, and simple
syrup.
3. Shake well.

4. Strain into a chilled cocktail glass.

5. Garnish with a lime wheel or twist.

Simplified Cooking From The 1930s With Pictures: The Era Of The Great Depression Recipes for Tenacity and Grit Made Easy

Simplified Cooking From The 1930s With Pictures: The Era Of The Great Depression Recipes for Tenacity and Grit Made Easy

Zombie

The Zombie is a legendary tiki cocktail known
for its exotic and complex flavors. It's a blend of
various rums, fruit juices, and spices that pack a
punch, often described as a "killer" cocktail.

Prep Time: 10 minutes Cook Time: 0 minutes
Servings: 1

Calories: 226 Fat: 0g Carbs: 13g Fiber: 0g
Sugar: 12g Protein: 0g

Ingredients:
- 1 1/2 oz light rum
- 1 1/2 oz dark rum
- 1 oz apricot brandy
- 1 oz lime juice
- 1 oz pineapple juice
- 1 oz orange juice
- 1/2 oz grenadine
- 1 dash of bitters
- Crushed ice
- Fresh fruit or mint sprig for garnish

Instructions:

1. Fill a shaker with ice.

2. Add all the ingredients (except garnish).

3. Shake vigorously.

4. Strain into a tiki glass filled with crushed ice.

5. Garnish with fresh fruit or a mint sprig.

Simplified Cooking From The 1930s With Pictures: The Era Of The Great Depression Recipes for Tenacity and Grit Made Easy

Simplified Cooking From The 1930s With Pictures: The Era Of The Great Depression Recipes for Tenacity and Grit Made Easy

Between the Sheets

This classic cocktail is a delightful mix of rum, cognac, and citrus flavors. It's a sophisticated and balanced drink that's perfect for those who appreciate a bit of elegance in their cocktails.

Prep Time: 5 minutes Cook Time: 0 minutes
Servings: 1

Calories: 183 Fat: 0g Carbs: 4g Fiber: 0g
Sugar: 2g Protein: 0g

Ingredients:
- 1 oz white rum
- 1 oz cognac
- 1 oz triple sec (orange liqueur)
- 3/4 oz fresh lemon juice
- Lemon twist for garnish

Instructions:
1. Fill a shaker with ice.

2. Add white rum, cognac, triple sec, and fresh lemon juice.

3. Shake well.

4. Strain into a chilled cocktail glass.

5. Garnish with a lemon twist.

Simplified Cooking From The 1930s With Pictures: The Era Of The Great Depression Recipes for Tenacity and Grit Made Easy

Simplified Cooking From The 1930s With Pictures: The Era Of The Great Depression Recipes for Tenacity and Grit Made Easy

Monkey Gland

The Monkey Gland cocktail is a classic from the 1930s known for its fruity and tangy flavors. It's named after a surgical procedure involving monkey testicles, but don't worry, there are no monkey parts in this drink!

Prep Time: 5 minutes Cook Time: 0 minutes Servings: 1

Calories: 150 Fat: 0g Carbs: 11g Fiber: 0g Sugar: 8g Protein: 0g

Ingredients:
2 oz gin
1 oz orange juice
1 dash grenadine syrup
1 dash absinthe

Instructions:
1. Fill a shaker with ice.
2. Pour in the gin, orange juice, and grenadine syrup.

3. Shake well and strain into a chilled cocktail glass rinsed with absinthe.

Simplified Cooking From The 1930s With Pictures: The Era Of The Great Depression Recipes for Tenacity and Grit Made Easy

Maryland Cocktail

The Maryland Cocktail is a timeless classic
with a blend of sweet and sour flavors, perfect
for those who enjoy a balanced cocktail
experience.

Prep Time: 5 minutes Cook Time: 0 minutes
Servings: 1

Calories: 160 Fat: 0g Carbs: 13g Fiber: 0g
Sugar: 12g Protein: 0g

Ingredients:
- 2 oz rye whiskey
- 1 oz orange juice
- 1 dash grenadine syrup

Instructions:
1. Fill a shaker with ice.
2. Pour in the rye whiskey, orange juice, and
grenadine syrup.
3. Shake well and strain into a chilled cocktail
glass.

Simplified Cooking From The 1930s With Pictures: The Era Of The Great Depression Recipes for Tenacity and Grit Made Easy

Simplified Cooking From The 1930s With Pictures: The Era Of The Great Depression Recipes for Tenacity and Grit Made Easy

Pink Lady

The Pink Lady cocktail is a delightful and
frothy concoction that became popular in the
1930s. It's known for its pretty pink color and a
sweet, slightly tart taste.

Prep Time: 5 minutes Cook Time: 0 minutes
Servings: 1

Calories: 190 Fat: 0g Carbs: 12g Fiber: 0g
Sugar: 11g Protein: 0g

Ingredients:
- 2 oz gin
- 1 oz applejack brandy
- 1 oz lemon juice
- 1 dash grenadine syrup
- 1 egg white

Instructions:
1. Fill a shaker with ice.
2. Pour in the gin, applejack brandy, lemon
juice, grenadine syrup, and egg white.

3. Shake vigorously without ice, then add ice and shake again.

4. Strain into a chilled cocktail glass.

Simplified Cooking From The 1930s With Pictures: The Era Of The Great Depression Recipes for Tenacity and Grit Made Easy

Scofflaw Cocktail

The Scofflaw is a cocktail that was created
during the era of Prohibition in the 1930s. It's a
delicious blend of rye whiskey, vermouth, and a
hint of citrus and grenadine, creating a well
balanced and flavorful drink.

Calories: 180 Fat: 0g Carbs: 10g Fiber: 0g
Sugar: 7g Protein: 0g

Prep Time: 5 minutes Cook Time: 0 minutes
Servings: 1 cocktail

Ingredients:
- 2 oz rye whiskey
- 1 oz dry vermouth
- 0.5 oz lemon juice
- 0.5 oz grenadine
- Dash of orange bitters
- Ice cubes

Instructions:

1. Fill a cocktail shaker with ice.

2. Add the rye whiskey, dry vermouth, lemon juice, grenadine, and a dash of orange bitters to the shaker.

3. Shake well until the mixture is wellchilled.

4. Strain the cocktail into a chilled cocktail glass.

5. Garnish with a lemon twist or cherry if desired.

Simplified Cooking From The 1930s With Pictures: The Era Of The Great Depression Recipes for Tenacity and Grit Made Easy

Simplified Cooking From The 1930s With Pictures: The Era Of The Great Depression Recipes for Tenacity and Grit Made Easy

Melon Ball

The Melon Ball is a refreshing and fruity
cocktail from the 1930s. It's known for its
vibrant green color and sweet melon flavor.

Prep Time: 5 minutes Servings: 1

Calories: 220 Fat: 0g Carbs: 18g Fiber: 0g
Sugar: 15g

Ingredients:
- 2 oz Midori melon liqueur
- 1 oz vodka
- 2 oz freshsqueezed orange juice
- Melon ball or slice for garnish

Instructions:
1. Fill a shaker with ice.
2. Add Midori, vodka, and orange juice to the
shaker.
3. Shake well and strain into a chilled cocktail
glass.

4. Garnish with a melon ball or slice on a cocktail pick.

Simplified Cooking From The 1930s With Pictures: The Era Of The Great Depression Recipes for Tenacity and Grit Made Easy

Simplified Cooking From The 1930s With Pictures: The
Era Of The Great Depression Recipes for Tenacity and
Grit Made Easy

Bacardi Cocktail

The Bacardi Cocktail is a classic cocktail from the 1930s known for its simplicity and refreshing taste. It features the iconic Bacardi rum, balanced with the zesty flavors of lime and grenadine.

Prep Time: 5 minutes Servings: 1

Calories: 120 Fat: 0g Carbs: 10g Fiber: 0g Sugar: 8g Protein: 0g

Ingredients:
- 2 oz Bacardi Superior Rum
- 1 oz freshly squeezed lime juice
- 1/2 oz grenadine syrup
- Ice cubes

Instructions:
1. Fill a cocktail shaker with ice.
2. Add Bacardi Superior Rum, freshly squeezed lime juice, and grenadine syrup to the shaker.

3. Shake well until chilled and strain the mixture into a chilled cocktail glass.

4. Garnish with a lime wheel or cherry if desired.

5. Serve and enjoy your classic Bacardi Cocktail from the 1930s!

Simplified Cooking From The 1930s With Pictures: The Era Of The Great Depression Recipes for Tenacity and Grit Made Easy

Simplified Cooking From The 1930s With Pictures: The Era Of The Great Depression Recipes for Tenacity and Grit Made Easy

Sloe Gin Fizz

The Sloe Gin Fizz is a refreshing and fruity cocktail that gained popularity in the 1930s. It features the sweet and tart flavors of sloe gin, balanced with the effervescence of soda water. This delightful drink is perfect for a warm summer day.

Prep Time: 5 minutes Servings: 1

Calories: 165 Fat: 0g Carbs: 14g Fiber: 0g Sugar: 12g Protein: 0g

Ingredients:
- 2 oz Sloe Gin
- 1 oz Fresh Lemon Juice
- 1/2 oz Simple Syrup
- 2 oz Club Soda
- Ice

Instructions:

1. Fill a cocktail shaker with ice.

2. Add Sloe Gin, fresh lemon juice, and simple syrup to the shaker.

3. Shake well until the mixture is chilled.

4. Strain the mixture into a highball glass filled with ice.

5. Top off with club soda.

6. Stir gently.

7. Garnish with a lemon slice or cherry if desired.

Simplified Cooking From The 1930s With Pictures: The Era Of The Great Depression Recipes for Tenacity and Grit Made Easy

Simplified Cooking From The 1930s With Pictures: The Era Of The Great Depression Recipes for Tenacity and Grit Made Easy

APPETIZERS

Angel Eggs

Angel eggs are a classic appetizer that consists of hard boiled eggs halved and filled with a flavorful, spiced yolk mixture.

Prep time: 15 minutes Cook time: 10 minutes Servings: 6

Calories: 90 Fat: 7g Carbs: 1g Fiber: 0g Sugar: 0g Protein: 6g

Ingredients:
- 6 large eggs
- 2 tablespoons mayonnaise
- 1 teaspoon Dijon mustard
- 1/2 teaspoon paprika
- Salt and pepper to taste
- Chopped fresh parsley for garnish

Instructions:
1. Place the eggs in a pot and cover with cold water. Bring to a boil, then reduce the heat and simmer for 10 minutes.
2. Remove the eggs, cool them in cold water, and peel.
3. Cut the eggs in half lengthwise and remove the yolks.
4. Mash the yolks and mix with mayonnaise, mustard, paprika, salt, and pepper.
5. Fill the egg whites with the yolk mixture.
6. Garnish with chopped parsley.
7. Serve and enjoy!

Simplified Cooking From The 1930s With Pictures: The
Era Of The Great Depression Recipes for Tenacity and
Grit Made Easy

Simplified Cooking From The 1930s With Pictures: The Era Of The Great Depression Recipes for Tenacity and Grit Made Easy

Shrimp Cocktail

Shrimp cocktail is a classic cold appetizer
featuring chilled cooked shrimp served with a
zesty cocktail sauce.

Prep time: 15 minutes Cook time: 5 minutes
Servings: 4

Calories: 120 Fat: 1g Carbs: 8g Fiber: 0g
Sugar: 6g Protein: 20g

Ingredients:
- 1 pound large shrimp, peeled and
  deveined
- 1 lemon, cut into wedges
- Ice for serving

For Cocktail Sauce:

- 1/2 cup ketchup

- 2 tablespoons horseradish
- 1 tablespoon Worcestershire sauce
- 1 teaspoon hot sauce (adjust to taste)
- Salt and pepper to taste

Instructions:

1. Fill a large pot with water and bring it to a boil.

2. Add the shrimp and cook for about 35 minutes until they turn pink and opaque.

3. Drain and place shrimp in a bowl with ice to cool.

4. In a separate bowl, mix together all the ingredients for the cocktail sauce.

5. Serve the chilled shrimp on a bed of ice with lemon wedges and cocktail sauce.

6. Enjoy this refreshing 1930s classic!

Simplified Cooking From The 1930s With Pictures: The Era Of The Great Depression Recipes for Tenacity and Grit Made Easy

Simplified Cooking From The 1930s With Pictures: The Era Of The Great Depression Recipes for Tenacity and Grit Made Easy

Stuffed Mushrooms

Stuffed mushrooms are a classic appetizer
where mushroom caps are filled with a savory
mixture and baked to perfection.

Prep time: 15 minutes Cook time: 20 minutes
Servings: 4

Calories: 80 Fat: 5g Carbs: 6g Fiber: 1g
Sugar: 1g Protein: 3g

Ingredients:
- 12 large mushrooms
- 1/4 cup breadcrumbs
- 1/4 cup grated Parmesan cheese
- 2 cloves garlic, minced
- 2 tablespoons fresh parsley, chopped
- 2 tablespoons olive oil
- Salt and pepper to taste

Instructions:
1. Preheat your oven to 350°F (175°C).
2. Clean the mushrooms and remove the stems.

3. In a bowl, mix breadcrumbs, Parmesan cheese, garlic, parsley, olive oil, salt, and pepper.

4. Stuff each mushroom cap with the mixture.

5. Place the stuffed mushrooms on a baking sheet and bake for about 20 minutes until they are golden brown.

Simplified Cooking From The 1930s With Pictures: The Era Of The Great Depression Recipes for Tenacity and Grit Made Easy

Simplified Cooking From The 1930s With Pictures: The Era Of The Great Depression Recipes for Tenacity and Grit Made Easy

Welsh Rarebit

Welsh Rarebit is a classic British dish, consisting of a savory cheese sauce served over toasted bread.

Prep time: 10 minutes Cook time: 10 minutes Servings: 2

Calories: 450 Fat: 30g Carbs: 20g Fiber: 1g Sugar: 1g Protein: 20g

Ingredients:

4 slices of bread

2 cups grated cheddar cheese

1 tablespoon butter

1 teaspoon Dijon mustard

1/2 cup ale or beer

1 egg yolk

Salt and cayenne pepper to taste

Instructions:

1. Toast the bread slices and set them aside.

2. In a saucepan, melt the butter, then add the mustard, cheese, and beer. Stir until the cheese is completely melted and the mixture is smooth.

3. Beat the egg yolk and add it to the cheese mixture, stirring well.

4. Season with salt and a pinch of cayenne pepper.

5. Pour the cheese sauce over the toasted bread slices.

Simplified Cooking From The 1930s With Pictures: The Era Of The Great Depression Recipes for Tenacity and Grit Made Easy

Oysters Rockefeller from the 1930s

Oysters Rockefeller is a classic appetizer known for its rich and flavorful topping. It originated in the 1930s and is traditionally made with oysters topped with a rich, green sauce and baked to perfection. Here's how you can prepare it:

Prep time: 15 minutes Cook time: 10 minutes
Servings: 4

Calories: 250 Fat: 18g Carbs: 12g Fiber: 2g
Sugar: 2g Protein: 12g

Ingredients:
- 24 fresh oysters on the half shell
- 1 cup fresh spinach, chopped
- 1/2 cup fresh parsley, chopped
- 1/4 cup green onions, chopped
- 1/4 cup celery, chopped
- 1/4 cup butter
- 1/4 cup breadcrumbs

- 1/4 cup grated Parmesan cheese
- 1/4 cup aniseflavored liqueur (e.g., Pernod)
- 1/4 teaspoon salt
- 1/4 teaspoon black pepper
- Crushed ice (for serving)

Instructions:

1. Preheat your oven to 450°F (230°C).

2. In a skillet, melt the butter over medium heat. Add spinach, parsley, green onions, and celery. Cook until wilted, about 34 minutes.

3. Stir in the breadcrumbs, Parmesan cheese, anise flavored liqueur, salt, and black pepper. Cook for an additional 2 minutes, until the mixture thickens.

4. Place the oysters on a bed of crushed ice on a baking sheet.

5. Spoon the spinach mixture over each oyster, covering them generously.

6. Bake in the preheated oven for about 10 minutes or until the topping is lightly browned and bubbling.

7. Serve hot and enjoy this classic 1930s appetizer, Oysters Rockefeller!

Simplified Cooking From The 1930s With Pictures: The Era Of The Great Depression Recipes for Tenacity and Grit Made Easy

Simplified Cooking From The 1930s With Pictures: The Era Of The Great Depression Recipes for Tenacity and Grit Made Easy

Rumaki

Rumaki is a popular 1930s appetizer that
features water chestnuts and chicken livers
wrapped in bacon, creating a delightful
combination of sweet, savory, and smoky
flavors.

Prep Time: 20 minutes Cook Time: 10 minutes
Servings: 4

Calories: 150 Fat: 8g Carbs: 5g Fiber: 1g
Sugar: 2g Protein: 12g

Ingredients:
- 16 chicken livers
- 8 water chestnuts, sliced into 16 pieces
- 8 slices of bacon, cut in half
- 16 toothpicks

Instructions:
1. Preheat the oven to 375°F (190°C).

2. Wrap each chicken liver and water chestnut slice with a halfslice of bacon and secure with a toothpick.

3. Place the rumaki on a baking sheet and bake for 10 minutes or until the bacon is crispy.

4. Serve hot and enjoy!

Simplified Cooking From The 1930s With Pictures: The Era Of The Great Depression Recipes for Tenacity and Grit Made Easy

Simplified Cooking From The 1930s With Pictures: The Era Of The Great Depression Recipes for Tenacity and Grit Made Easy

Lobster Newberg

Lobster Newberg is a luxurious 1930s dish featuring tender lobster meat in a rich, creamy sauce with a hint of sherry and egg yolks, often served over toast points or in a pastry shell.

Prep Time: 30 minutes Cook Time: 20 minutes Servings: 2

Calories: 380 Fat: 22g Carbs: 8g Fiber: 0g Sugar: 3g Protein: 36g

Ingredients:
- 2 lobster tails, cooked and meat removed
- 2 tablespoons butter
- 2 tablespoons brandy or sherry
- 2 egg yolks
- 1 cup heavy cream
- Salt and cayenne pepper to taste
- Toast points or pastry shells for serving

Instructions:

1. In a pan, melt the butter and add the lobster meat. Cook briefly.

2. Add the brandy or sherry and ignite to flambe. Be careful while doing this step.

3. In a separate bowl, beat the egg yolks and stir in the heavy cream.

4. Slowly add the egg and cream mixture to the lobster, stirring constantly until the sauce thickens.

5. Season with salt and cayenne pepper to taste.

6. Serve the Lobster Newberg over toast points or in pastry shells.

Simplified Cooking From The 1930s With Pictures: The Era Of The Great Depression Recipes for Tenacity and Grit Made Easy

Simplified Cooking From The 1930s With Pictures: The Era Of The Great Depression Recipes for Tenacity and Grit Made Easy

Crab Rangoon

Crab Rangoon is a popular appetizer made with a crispy wonton wrapper filled with a creamy mixture of crab meat and cream cheese.

Prep Time: 20 minutes Cook Time: 15 minutes Servings: 4

Calories: 180 Fat: 11g Carbs: 15g Fiber: 1g Sugar: 2g Protein: 6g

Ingredients:
- 8 oz crab meat
- 8 oz cream cheese
- 1/4 cup green onions, chopped
- 1/4 tsp Worcestershire sauce
- 1/4 tsp soy sauce
- 1 package wonton wrappers
- Oil for frying

Instructions:

1. In a bowl, combine crab meat, cream cheese, green onions, Worcestershire sauce, and soy sauce.

2. Place a small spoonful of the mixture in the center of each wonton wrapper.

3. Moisten the edges of the wrapper with water, then fold it in half to form a triangle and press to seal.

4. Heat oil in a pan, and fry the crab Rangoon until golden brown.

5. Drain on paper towels and serve hot.

Simplified Cooking From The 1930s With Pictures: The Era Of The Great Depression Recipes for Tenacity and Grit Made Easy

Simplified Cooking From The 1930s With Pictures: The Era Of The Great Depression Recipes for Tenacity and Grit Made Easy

Cucumber Sandwiches

Cucumber sandwiches are delicate finger sandwiches consisting of thinly sliced cucumbers, butter, and sometimes cream cheese between slices of white bread.

Prep Time: 10 minutes Cook Time: 0 minutes
Servings: 6

Calories: 90 Fat: 5g Carbs: 9g Fiber: 1g
Sugar: 1g Protein: 2g

Ingredients:
- 1 cucumber, thinly sliced
- 12 slices of white bread
- Butter or cream cheese

Instructions:
1. Trim the crusts from the bread slices.
2. Spread a thin layer of butter or cream cheese on each slice.
3. Place cucumber slices on half of the bread slices.

4. Top with the remaining slices to make sandwiches.

5. Cut the sandwiches into smaller, bitesized pieces, and serve.

Simplified Cooking From The 1930s With Pictures: The Era Of The Great Depression Recipes for Tenacity and Grit Made Easy

Stuffed Celery

Stuffed celery is a classic appetizer where celery sticks are filled with a seasoned cream cheese or peanut butter mixture, creating a satisfying and crunchy bite.

Prep Time: 15 minutes Cook Time: 0 minutes
Servings: 8

Calories: 70 Fat: 5g Carbs: 4g Fiber: 1g Sugar: 2g Protein: 2g

Ingredients:
- 16 celery sticks
- 8 oz cream cheese or peanut butter
- 1/4 cup chopped nuts (optional)
- Salt and pepper to taste

Instructions:
1. Wash and trim the celery sticks to the desired length.

2. In a bowl, mix the cream cheese or peanut butter with chopped nuts (if using), salt, and pepper.

3. Fill the celery sticks with the mixture.

4. Serve as individual sticks or arrange them on a platter. Enjoy!

Simplified Cooking From The 1930s With Pictures: The Era Of The Great Depression Recipes for Tenacity and Grit Made Easy

Simplified Cooking From The 1930s With Pictures: The Era Of The Great Depression Recipes for Tenacity and Grit Made Easy

Fruit Cocktail

A classic 1930s appetizer, fruit cocktail is a delightful mix of canned fruits served in a sweet syrup.

Prep Time: 10 minutes Cook Time: 0 minutes
Servings: 4

Calories: 120 Fat: 0g Carbs: 30g Fiber: 2g
Sugar: 28g Protein: 1g

Ingredients:
- 1 can (15 oz) fruit cocktail
- 1 tablespoon lemon juice
- 2 tablespoons honey
- 1/4 teaspoon ground cinnamon
- Maraschino cherries for garnish (optional)

Instructions:
1. Drain the fruit cocktail and transfer it to a bowl.

2. In a separate bowl, mix lemon juice, honey, and cinnamon.

3. Pour the honey mixture over the fruit and gently toss to coat.

4. Garnish with maraschino cherries if desired.

5. Chill in the refrigerator for 30 minutes before serving.

Simplified Cooking From The 1930s With Pictures: The Era Of The Great Depression Recipes for Tenacity and Grit Made Easy

Baked Brie

Baked Brie is an elegant 1930s appetizer,
featuring a wheel of creamy Brie cheese baked
until it's soft and gooey, often topped with nuts
or preserves.

Prep Time: 15 minute Cook Time: 20 minutes
Servings: 6

Calories: 220 Fat: 18g Carbs: 2g Fiber: 0g
Sugar: 1g Protein: 12g

Ingredients:
1 wheel of Brie cheese
1/4 cup chopped nuts (e.g., almonds or walnuts)
2 tablespoons fruit preserves (e.g., apricot or
raspberry)
1 French baguette, sliced

Instructions:

1. Preheat the oven to 350°F (175°C).

2. Place the Brie wheel in a small baking dish.

3. Sprinkle the chopped nuts over the Brie.

4. Heat the fruit preserves in a microwave for 20 seconds, then drizzle over the Brie.

5. Bake in the preheated oven for about 20 minutes or until the Brie is soft and gooey.

6. Serve with sliced French baguette.

Simplified Cooking From The 1930s With Pictures: The Era Of The Great Depression Recipes for Tenacity and Grit Made Easy

Simplified Cooking From The 1930s With Pictures: The Era Of The Great Depression Recipes for Tenacity and Grit Made Easy

Vegetable Platter with Dip

This 1930s vegetable platter is a refreshing and
healthy appetizer featuring a variety of fresh,
crunchy vegetables served with a tangy dip.

Prep Time: 20 minutes Cook Time: 0 minutes
Servings: 8

Calories: 60 Fat: 4g Carbs: 6g Fiber: 2g
Sugar: 2g Protein: 2g

Ingredients:
- Assorted fresh vegetables (e.g., carrots,
  celery, bell peppers, cherry tomatoes,
  cucumber)
- For the Dip:
- 1 cup Greek yogurt
- 2 tablespoons mayonnaise
- 1 teaspoon lemon juice
- 1 teaspoon chopped fresh dill
- Salt and pepper to taste

Instructions:
1. Wash and cut the fresh vegetables into bitesized sticks or slices.
2. Arrange the vegetables on a serving platter.
3. In a small bowl, mix Greek yogurt, mayonnaise, lemon juice, dill, salt, and pepper to create the dip.
4. Serve the vegetables with the dip on the side.

Simplified Cooking From The 1930s With Pictures: The Era Of The Great Depression Recipes for Tenacity and Grit Made Easy

Simplified Cooking From The 1930s With Pictures: The Era Of The Great Depression Recipes for Tenacity and Grit Made Easy

Rice Pudding

Prep Time: 15 minutes Cook Time: 90 minutes
Servings: 6

Calories: 250 Fat: 6g Carbs: 45g Fiber: 0g
Sugar: 20g Protein: 6g

A classic comfort dessert made from rice, milk,
sugar, and a hint of vanilla. It's slowcooked to a
creamy perfection.

Ingredients:
- 1 cup of rice
- 4 cups of milk
- 1/2 cup of sugar
- 1 teaspoon of vanilla extract

Instructions:
1. Rinse the rice and combine it with milk in a
saucepan.
2. Add sugar and vanilla, then bring to a
simmer.

3. Cook on low heat, stirring often, until the rice is soft and the mixture thickens.

4. Serve warm or cold.

Simplified Cooking From The 1930s With Pictures: The Era Of The Great Depression Recipes for Tenacity and Grit Made Easy

Simplified Cooking From The 1930s With Pictures: The Era Of The Great Depression Recipes for Tenacity and Grit Made Easy

Bread Pudding

Prep Time: 20 minutes Cook Time: 45 minutes
Servings: 8

Calories: 320 Fat: 10g Carbs: 50g Fiber: 1g
Sugar: 30g Protein: 10g

A thrifty and delicious dessert that repurposes stale bread, combining it with eggs, milk, sugar, and spices, then baking to a golden brown.

Ingredients:
- 4 cups of stale bread, cubed
- 2 cups of milk
- 3/4 cup of sugar
- 2 eggs
- 1 teaspoon of vanilla extract

Instructions:
1. Preheat the oven to 350°F (175°C).
2. In a bowl, mix bread, milk, and sugar. Let it sit for 15 minutes.

3. Beat eggs and vanilla, then add to the bread mixture.

4. Pour the mixture into a greased baking dish and bake until golden and set.

5. Serve warm with a sprinkle of sugar or a dollop of whipped cream.

Simplified Cooking From The 1930s With Pictures: The Era Of The Great Depression Recipes for Tenacity and Grit Made Easy

Simplified Cooking From The 1930s With Pictures: The Era Of The Great Depression Recipes for Tenacity and Grit Made Easy

Jello

Prep Time: 5 minutes Servings: 4

Calories: 80 Fat: 0g Carbs: 20g Fiber: 0g
Sugar: 20g Protein: 2g

A wobbly, colorful dessert made from fruit
flavored gelatin. It became an iconic treat in the
1930s, especially with creative molds and fruit
additions.

Ingredients:
- 1 package of fruitflavored gelatin
- 2 cups of boiling water

Instructions:
1. Dissolve the gelatin in boiling water.
2. Pour the mixture into molds or a glass dish.
3. Refrigerate until it's set.
4. Serve chilled with optional fruit garnish.

Simplified Cooking From The 1930s With Pictures: The Era Of The Great Depression Recipes for Tenacity and Grit Made Easy

Apple Crisp

Prep Time: 15 minutes Cook Time: 40 minutes
Servings: 6

Calories: 220 Fat: 7g Carbs: 40g Fiber: 4g
Sugar: 20g Protein: 2g

A warm dessert consisting of baked apples with
a crispy, sweet oat topping. It was a popular way
to use seasonal apples during the 1930s.

Ingredients:
- 4 cups of sliced apples
- 1/2 cup of rolled oats
- 1/2 cup of brown sugar
- 1/4 cup of butter
- 1 teaspoon of cinnamon

Instructions:
1. Preheat the oven to 350°F (175°C).
2. Place sliced apples in a baking dish.
3. In a separate bowl, mix oats, brown sugar,
butter, and cinnamon until crumbly.

4. Sprinkle the oat mixture over the apples.

5. Bake until the topping is golden and the apples are tender.

6. Serve warm with a scoop of ice cream or a drizzle of caramel.

Simplified Cooking From The 1930s With Pictures: The Era Of The Great Depression Recipes for Tenacity and Grit Made Easy

Simplified Cooking From The 1930s With Pictures: The Era Of The Great Depression Recipes for Tenacity and Grit Made Easy

The Depression Cake

The Depression Cake, also known as Wacky
Cake, is a simple and economical dessert that
originated during the Great Depression. It
doesn't require eggs or dairy due to ingredient
scarcity during that era.

Calories: 180 Fat: 5g Carbs: 34g Fiber: 2g
Sugar: 18g Protein: 3g

Ingredients:

- 1 1/2 cups allpurpose flour
- 1 cup sugar
- 1/4 cup unsweetened cocoa powder
- 1 tsp baking soda
- 1/2 tsp salt
- 1 tsp white vinegar
- 1 tsp pure vanilla extract
- 5 tbsp vegetable oil
- 1 cup water

Instructions:

1. Preheat your oven to 350°F (175°C).

2. In an ungreased 8inch square baking pan, sift together the flour, sugar, cocoa powder, baking soda, and salt.

3. Make three depressions in the dry ingredients – two small and one large. Pour the vinegar and vanilla extract into the small depressions and the vegetable oil into the large one.

4. Pour water over everything and stir well until smooth.

5. Bake for 30 to 40 minutes, or until a toothpick inserted into the cake comes out clean.

Simplified Cooking From The 1930s With Pictures: The Era Of The Great Depression Recipes for Tenacity and Grit Made Easy

Simplified Cooking From The 1930s With Pictures: The
Era Of The Great Depression Recipes for Tenacity and
Grit Made Easy

Ambrosia Salad

Ambrosia Salad is a classic Southern dessert
salad featuring a combination of citrus fruits,
coconut, and sometimes marshmallows, bound
together with a creamy dressing.

Calories: 230 Fat: 8g Carbs: 40g Fiber: 4g
Sugar: 30g Protein: 2g

Ingredients:

- 2 cups canned pineapple chunks,
  drained
- 1 cup mandarin oranges, drained
- 1 cup shredded coconut
- 1 cup miniature marshmallows
- 1 cup sour cream
- 1 cup whipped topping

Instructions:

1. In a large bowl, combine the pineapple, mandarin oranges, coconut, and marshmallows.

2. Gently fold in the sour cream and whipped topping until well mixed.

3. Chill in the refrigerator for at least 1 hour before serving.

Simplified Cooking From The 1930s With Pictures: The Era Of The Great Depression Recipes for Tenacity and Grit Made Easy

Simplified Cooking From The 1930s With Pictures: The Era Of The Great Depression Recipes for Tenacity and Grit Made Easy

Date Nut Bread

Date Nut Bread is a sweet and dense bread
made with dates and chopped nuts. It was a
popular choice during the 1930s and often
served with butter or cream cheese.

Calories: 180 Fat: 7g Carbs: 28g   Fiber: 3g
Sugar: 16g Protein: 3g

Ingredients:
- 1 cup chopped dates
- 1 cup chopped nuts (e.g., walnuts)
- 1 cup boiling water
- 1 tsp baking soda
- 1 cup sugar
- 2 tbsp butter
- 1 egg
- 2 cups allpurpose flour
- 1 tsp vanilla extract
- A pinch of salt

Instructions:
1. Preheat your oven to 350°F (175°C).

2. In a mixing bowl, pour boiling water over the dates and baking soda. Let it cool.

3. Cream together sugar, butter, and egg. Add the date mixture and mix well.

4. Stir in flour, nuts, vanilla extract, and a pinch of salt until just combined.

5. Pour the batter into a greased and floured loaf pan.

6. Bake for approximately 60 minutes or until a toothpick comes out clean.

Simplified Cooking From The 1930s With Pictures: The Era Of The Great Depression Recipes for Tenacity and Grit Made Easy

Simplified Cooking From The 1930s With Pictures: The Era Of The Great Depression Recipes for Tenacity and Grit Made Easy

Chocolate Mayonnaise Cake

Chocolate Mayonnaise Cake was a creative
way to use mayonnaise as a substitute for eggs
and oil during the Great Depression. The
mayonnaise adds moisture to the cake.

Calories: 280 Fat: 14g Carbs: 36g Fiber: 2g
Sugar: 20g Protein: 4g

Ingredients:

1 1/2 cups allpurpose flour

1/4 cup unsweetened cocoa powder

1 1/2 tsp baking soda

3/4 cup sugar

1 cup mayonnaise

1 cup cold water

1 tsp pure vanilla extract

Instructions:

1. Preheat your oven to 350°F (175°C).

2. Grease and flour two 9inch round cake pans.

3. In a large mixing bowl, combine the flour,
cocoa powder, baking soda, and sugar.

4. Add mayonnaise, cold water, and vanilla extract. Beat until well mixed.

5. Pour the batter evenly into the prepared pans.

6. Bake for about 35 minutes or until a toothpick inserted into the center comes out clean.

Simplified Cooking From The 1930s With Pictures: The Era Of The Great Depression Recipes for Tenacity and Grit Made Easy

Simplified Cooking From The 1930s With Pictures: The
Era Of The Great Depression Recipes for Tenacity and
Grit Made Easy

Pineapple UpsideDown Cake

Pineapple UpsideDown Cake is a delightful dessert where caramelized pineapple slices and cherries are placed at the bottom of a cake pan, and a buttery cake batter is poured on top, then baked and inverted for serving.

Ingredients:

- 1/4 cup butter
- 2/3 cup packed brown sugar
- 1 can (20 oz) pineapple slices in juice, drained, juice reserved
- Maraschino cherries
- 1 1/3 cups allpurpose flour
- 1 cup granulated sugar
- 1/3 cup vegetable oil
- 1 1/2 tsp baking powder
- 1/2 tsp salt
- 1/2 cup milk
- 1 tsp vanilla extract
- 1 large egg

Instructions:

1. Preheat your oven to 350°F (175°C).

2. Melt butter in a 9x9inch square baking pan in the preheated oven.

3. Sprinkle brown sugar evenly over the melted butter.

4. Arrange pineapple slices and cherries over the brown sugar.

5. In a mixing bowl, whisk together flour, granulated sugar, baking powder, and salt.

6. Add reserved pineapple juice, vegetable oil, milk, vanilla extract.

Simplified Cooking From The 1930s With Pictures: The Era Of The Great Depression Recipes for Tenacity and Grit Made Easy

Simplified Cooking From The 1930s With Pictures: The Era Of The Great Depression Recipes for Tenacity and Grit Made Easy

Molasses Cookies

Molasses cookies are a classic, chewy treat
with a rich, sweet flavor thanks to molasses and
warm spices.

Ingredients:

- 1 cup molasses
- 3/4 cup shortening
- 2 1/4 cups allpurpose flour
- 1 tsp baking soda
- 1/2 tsp salt
- 1 1/2 tsp ground ginger
- 1 tsp ground cinnamon
- 1/2 tsp ground cloves
- Sugar for rolling

Instructions:

1. Preheat your oven to 350°F (175°C).

2. In a mixing bowl, combine molasses and
shortening.

3. In a separate bowl, mix the dry ingredients:
flour, baking soda, salt, ginger, cinnamon, and
cloves.

4. Gradually add the dry mixture to the molasses mixture and blend well.

5. Roll the dough into small balls, then roll them in sugar.

6. Place the dough balls on a greased baking sheet.

7. Bake for 10 minutes. Allow them to cool before serving.

Simplified Cooking From The 1930s With Pictures: The Era Of The Great Depression Recipes for Tenacity and Grit Made Easy

Simplified Cooking From The 1930s With Pictures: The
Era Of The Great Depression Recipes for Tenacity and
Grit Made Easy

Butterscotch Pudding

Butterscotch pudding is a creamy, caramel flavored dessert with a smooth texture that melts in your mouth.

Ingredients:

- 1 cup brown sugar
- 2 tbsp cornstarch
- 2 cups milk
- 2 egg yolks
- 2 tbsp butter
- 1 tsp vanilla extract

Instructions:

1. In a saucepan, mix brown sugar and cornstarch.

2. Gradually stir in the milk.

3. Cook over medium heat, stirring constantly until it thickens.

4. In a separate bowl, beat the egg yolks and gradually add a small amount of the hot sugar mixture.

5. Pour the egg mixture back into the saucepan and cook for 2 minutes, stirring constantly.

6. Remove from heat, add butter and vanilla, and stir until smooth.

7. Pour into serving dishes and chill before serving.

Simplified Cooking From The 1930s With Pictures: The Era Of The Great Depression Recipes for Tenacity and Grit Made Easy

Simplified Cooking From The 1930s With Pictures: The Era Of The Great Depression Recipes for Tenacity and Grit Made Easy

Raisin Pie

Raisin pie is a sweet and fruity pie made with plump raisins, sugar, and warm spices, all baked into a delicious crust.

Ingredients:

- 2 cups raisins
- 1 cup white sugar
- 1 tbsp all purpose flour
- 1/2 tsp salt
- 1/2 tsp ground cinnamon
- 1/4 tsp ground nutmeg
- 1 1/2 cups water
- 2 tbsp lemon juice
- 1 tbsp butter
- Pastry for a doublecrust pie

Instructions:

1. Preheat your oven to 425°F (220°C).

2. In a saucepan, combine raisins, sugar, flour, salt, cinnamon, nutmeg, water, and lemon juice.

3. Cook over medium heat until it thickens.

4. Remove from heat, stir in butter, and let it cool.

5. Line a pie pan with pastry, pour in the raisin filling, and cover with a top crust.

6. Bake for 15 minutes, then reduce the heat to 375°F (190°C) and bake for an additional 30 minutes.

Simplified Cooking From The 1930s With Pictures: The Era Of The Great Depression Recipes for Tenacity and Grit Made Easy

Shoofly Pie

Shoofly pie is a molasses based dessert with a
crumbly, sweet topping and a gooey, molasses
rich filling.

Ingredients:
- 1 cup molasses
- 1 cup hot water
- 1 tsp baking soda
- 1 1/2 cups allpurpose flour
- 1 cup brown sugar
- 1/2 cup shortening
- Pastry for a singlecrust pie

Instructions:
1. Preheat your oven to 425°F (220°C).
2. In a mixing bowl, combine molasses, hot
water, and baking soda.
3. In a separate bowl, mix flour and brown
sugar.

4. Cut in the shortening until the mixture resembles coarse crumbs.

5. Line a pie pan with pastry and pour in the molasses mixture.

6. Sprinkle the crumb mixture on top.

7. Bake for 15 minutes, then reduce the heat to 350°F (175°C) and bake for an additional 35 minutes.

Simplified Cooking From The 1930s With Pictures: The
Era Of The Great Depression Recipes for Tenacity and
Grit Made Easy

Simplified Cooking From The 1930s With Pictures: The
Era Of The Great Depression Recipes for Tenacity and
Grit Made Easy

MAIN DISH

Meatloaf

Meatloaf is a comforting dish made from
ground beef mixed with various ingredients and
seasonings, shaped into a loaf, and baked.

Prep time: 15 minutes Cook time: 1 hour
Servings: 6

Calories: 350 Fat: 20g Carbs: 15g Fiber: 2g
Sugar: 4g Protein: 25g

Ingredients:
- 1 1/2 pounds ground beef
- 1/2 cup breadcrumbs
- 1/4 cup milk
- 1/4 cup finely chopped onion
- 1/4 cup finely chopped bell pepper
- 1 egg
- 1 teaspoon salt
- 1/2 teaspoon black pepper
- 1/2 cup ketchup

Instructions:

1. Preheat your oven to 350°F (175°C).

2. In a large mixing bowl, combine ground beef, breadcrumbs, milk, onion, bell pepper, egg, salt, and black pepper.

3. Shape the mixture into a loaf and place it in a baking dish.

4. Spread ketchup over the top of the loaf.

5. Bake for 1 hour or until the internal temperature reaches 160°F (70°C).

Simplified Cooking From The 1930s With Pictures: The Era Of The Great Depression Recipes for Tenacity and Grit Made Easy

Simplified Cooking From The 1930s With Pictures: The Era Of The Great Depression Recipes for Tenacity and Grit Made Easy

Chicken à la King

Chicken à la King is a creamy dish featuring
chicken and bell peppers in a rich, sherryinfused
cream sauce, often served over toast or in a
pastry shell.

Prep time: 20 minutes Cook time: 30 minutes
Servings: 4

Calories: 400 Fat: 25g Carbs: 20g Fiber: 3g
Sugar: 6g   Protein: 20g

Ingredients:
- 2 cups cooked chicken, diced
- 1/4 cup butter
- 1/4 cup allpurpose flour
- 1 cup chicken broth
- 1 cup milk
- 1/4 cup sherry
- 1/2 cup diced bell peppers
- Salt and pepper to taste
- Toast or pastry shells for serving

Instructions:

1. Melt butter in a saucepan over medium heat. Stir in flour to make a roux.

2. Gradually whisk in chicken broth, milk, and sherry. Cook and stir until the sauce thickens.

3. Add diced chicken and bell peppers to the sauce. Cook until heated through.

4. Season with salt and pepper to taste.

5. Serve over toast or in pastry shells.

Simplified Cooking From The 1930s With Pictures: The Era Of The Great Depression Recipes for Tenacity and Grit Made Easy

Beef Stroganoff

Beef Stroganoff is a Russianinspired dish with
tender strips of beef, mushrooms, and onions in
a creamy sour cream sauce, typically served over
egg noodles.

Prep time: 10 minutes Cook time: 20 minutes
Servings: 4

Calories: 450 Fat: 30g Carbs: 15g Fiber: 2g
Sugar: 4g Protein: 25g

Ingredients:
- 1 pound beef sirloin, thinly sliced
- 1/2 cup onion, chopped
- 1 cup mushrooms, sliced
- 2 tablespoons butter
- 1 cup sour cream
- 2 tablespoons allpurpose flour
- 1 cup beef broth

- Salt and pepper to taste
- Cooked egg noodles for serving

Instructions:

1. In a skillet, melt the butter over medium heat. Add onions and mushrooms, sauté until tender.

2. Add beef slices and cook until browned. Remove from the skillet.

3. Stir flour into the skillet, then gradually add beef broth, stirring until thickened.

4. Return beef and vegetables to the skillet, and simmer for a few minutes.

5. Stir in sour cream and heat through without boiling.

6. Season with salt and pepper, and serve over cooked egg noodles.

Simplified Cooking From The 1930s With Pictures: The Era Of The Great Depression Recipes for Tenacity and Grit Made Easy

Simplified Cooking From The 1930s With Pictures: The Era Of The Great Depression Recipes for Tenacity and Grit Made Easy

Chicken Pot Pie

Chicken Pot Pie is a savory pie filled with
diced chicken, vegetables (such as peas and
carrots), and a creamy sauce, all encased in a
flaky pastry crust.

Prep time: 30 minutes Cook time: 45 minutes
Servings: 6

Calories: 350 Fat: 20g Carbs: 30g Fiber: 4g
Sugar: 4g Protein: 15g

Ingredients:

- 2 cups cooked chicken, diced
- 1 cup frozen mixed vegetables
- 1/2 cup diced potatoes
- 1/4 cup butter
- 1/3 cup chopped onion
- 1/3 cup allpurpose flour
- 1/2 teaspoon salt
- 1/4 teaspoon black pepper
- 1 3/4 cups chicken broth
- 2/3 cup milk

- 2 pie crusts (storebought or homemade)

Instructions:

1. Preheat your oven to 425°F (220°C).

2. In a saucepan, melt the butter over medium heat. Add onions and cook until translucent.

3. Stir in flour, salt, and black pepper. Gradually add chicken broth and milk. Cook and stir until the sauce thickens.

4. Add chicken, vegetables, and potatoes. Cook until the vegetables are tender.

5. Line a pie dish with one pie crust. Pour in the chicken mixture and cover with the second pie crust.

6. Bake for 45 minutes or until the crust is golden brown.

Simplified Cooking From The 1930s With Pictures: The Era Of The Great Depression Recipes for Tenacity and Grit Made Easy

Simplified Cooking From The 1930s With Pictures: The Era Of The Great Depression Recipes for Tenacity and Grit Made Easy

Deviled Ham

Deviled Ham is a spiced and seasoned ham
spread made from ground ham, often mixed with
mustard, mayonnaise, and other seasonings,
served as a sandwich filling or dip.

Prep time: 10 minutes Servings: 4

Calories: 150 Fat: 10g Carbs: 5g Fiber: 1g
Sugar: 2g Protein: 10g

Ingredients:
- 1 cup ground ham
- 2 tablespoons mayonnaise
- 1 teaspoon Dijon mustard
- 1/2 teaspoon paprika
- 1/4 teaspoon cayenne pepper
- Salt and pepper to taste

Instructions:
1. In a bowl, combine ground ham,
mayonnaise, Dijon mustard, paprika, and
cayenne pepper.

2. Mix well until the ingredients are fully incorporated.

3. Season with salt and pepper to taste.

4. Serve as a sandwich filling or as a dip with crackers.

Simplified Cooking From The 1930s With Pictures: The Era Of The Great Depression Recipes for Tenacity and Grit Made Easy

Simplified Cooking From The 1930s With Pictures: The
Era Of The Great Depression Recipes for Tenacity and
Grit Made Easy

Creamed Spinach

Creamed spinach is a classic side dish made with
spinach, butter, cream, and various seasonings,
offering a rich, creamy, and flavorful vegetable
accompaniment.

Servings: 4 Prep Time: 15 minutes Cook Time:
20 minutes

Calories: 120 Fat: 9g Carbs: 8g Fiber: 4g Sugar:
2g Protein: 4g

Ingredients:
- Spinach
- Butter
- Heavy cream
- Seasonings

Instructions (from the 1930s):
1. Wash and blanch the spinach.
2. Sauté the spinach in butter.

3. Add heavy cream and seasonings.

4. Simmer until thickened.

Simplified Cooking From The 1930s With Pictures: The Era Of The Great Depression Recipes for Tenacity and Grit Made Easy

Beef and Noodles

Beef and noodles is a hearty dish combining tender beef cuts with egg noodles, often cooked in a flavorsome broth or sauce.

Servings: 6 Prep Time: 20 minutes Cook Time: 90 minutes

Calories: 350 Fat: 14g Carbs: 32g Fiber: 3g Sugar: 2g Protein: 24g

Ingredients:
- Beef chunks
- Egg noodles
- Broth/stock
- Seasonings

Instructions (from the 1930s):
1. Brown beef chunks in a pot.
2. Add broth/stock and simmer until beef is tender.

3. Cook egg noodles separately.

4. Combine cooked noodles with the beef and broth mixture.

Simplified Cooking From The 1930s With Pictures: The Era Of The Great Depression Recipes for Tenacity and Grit Made Easy

Simplified Cooking From The 1930s With Pictures: The Era Of The Great Depression Recipes for Tenacity and Grit Made Easy

Tuna Noodle Casserole

Tuna noodle casserole is a baked dish made with
canned tuna, egg noodles, and a creamy sauce,
often topped with breadcrumbs or cheese.

Servings: 8 Prep Time: 25 minutes Cook Time:
35 minutes

Calories: 280 Fat: 10g Carbs: 28g Fiber: 3g
Sugar: 4g Protein: 18g

Ingredients:
- Canned tuna
- Egg noodles
- Cream of mushroom soup
- Peas (optional)
- Bread crumbs (for topping)

Instructions (from the 1930s):
1. Cook egg noodles and mix with canned tuna
and cream of mushroom soup.
2. Add peas if desired.

3. Place the mixture in a casserole dish and top with breadcrumbs.

4. Bake until bubbly and golden.

Simplified Cooking From The 1930s With Pictures: The Era Of The Great Depression Recipes for Tenacity and Grit Made Easy

Simplified Cooking From The 1930s With Pictures: The Era Of The Great Depression Recipes for Tenacity and Grit Made Easy

Liver and Onions

Liver and onions is a dish featuring thinly sliced liver cooked with onions, often panfried and seasoned for a robust flavor.

Servings: 4 Prep Time: 10 minutes Cook Time: 20 minutes

Calories: 280 Fat: 12g Carbs: 10g Fiber: 2g Sugar: 4g Protein: 30g

Ingredients:
- Beef liver
- Onions
- Flour (for coating)
- Seasonings

Instructions (from the 1930s):

1. Dredge liver slices in flour and seasonings.
2. Sauté liver and onions in a pan until cooked through.
3. Season to taste.

Simplified Cooking From The 1930s With Pictures: The Era Of The Great Depression Recipes for Tenacity and Grit Made Easy

Baked Ham with Pineapple

Baked ham with pineapple is a classic dish
where a ham is glazed and baked, often
garnished with pineapple slices for added
sweetness and flavor.

Servings: 10 Prep Time: 15 minutes Cook Time:
3 hours
Calories: 350 Fat: 18g Carbs: 15g Fiber: 1g
Sugar: 12g Protein: 30g

Ingredients:
- Ham
- Pineapple
- Brown sugar (for glaze)
- Cloves (optional)

Instructions (from the 1930s):
1. Score the ham and stud with cloves if desired.
2. Glaze the ham with a mixture of brown sugar
and pineapple juice.
3. Place pineapple slices around the ham.
4. Bake until fully cooked.

Simplified Cooking From The 1930s With Pictures: The Era Of The Great Depression Recipes for Tenacity and Grit Made Easy

Stuffed Bell Peppers

Ingredients:

- 4 large bell peppers
- 1 pound ground beef
- 1 cup cooked rice
- 1 onion, chopped
- 1 can (14 oz) diced tomatoes
- Salt, pepper, and other preferred seasonings

Instructions:

1. Preheat oven to 350°F.

2. Cut the tops off the bell peppers and remove seeds and membranes.

3. In a skillet, brown the ground beef with onions. Drain excess fat.

4. Mix cooked rice, diced tomatoes, and seasonings into the beef mixture.

5. Stuff each bell pepper with the mixture.

6. Place stuffed peppers in a baking dish and bake for 4550 minutes, until the peppers are tender.

Simplified Cooking From The 1930s With Pictures: The Era Of The Great Depression Recipes for Tenacity and Grit Made Easy

Simplified Cooking From The 1930s With Pictures: The Era Of The Great Depression Recipes for Tenacity and Grit Made Easy

Creamed Chipped Beef on Toast

Ingredients:

- 1/4 pound chipped beef, chopped
- 2 tablespoons butter
- 2 tablespoons allpurpose flour
- 2 cups milk
- Salt and pepper to taste
- Toast for serving

Instructions:

1. In a skillet, melt butter and add chopped chipped beef.

2. Stir in flour and cook for 12 minutes.

3. Gradually add milk, stirring constantly until the mixture thickens.

4. Season with salt and pepper to taste.

5. Serve the creamed chipped beef over toasted bread.

Simplified Cooking From The 1930s With Pictures: The Era Of The Great Depression Recipes for Tenacity and Grit Made Easy

Simplified Cooking From The 1930s With Pictures: The Era Of The Great Depression Recipes for Tenacity and Grit Made Easy

Chicken and Dumplings

Ingredients:

- 1 whole chicken, cut into pieces
- 4 cups chicken broth
- 2 carrots, sliced
- 2 celery stalks, sliced
- 1 onion, chopped
- 2 cups allpurpose flour
- 1 tablespoon baking powder
- 1/2 teaspoon salt
- 3/4 cup milk
- Herbs and seasonings of choice

Instructions:

1. In a large pot, combine chicken pieces, chicken broth, carrots, celery, onion, and preferred herbs. Simmer for 4550 minutes until the chicken is cooked.

2. In a bowl, mix flour, baking powder, salt, and milk to form a dough.

3. Drop spoonfuls of the dough into the simmering broth.

4. Cover and cook for 10 minutes until the dumplings are cooked through.

Simplified Cooking From The 1930s With Pictures: The
Era Of The Great Depression Recipes for Tenacity and
Grit Made Easy

Simplified Cooking From The 1930s With Pictures: The Era Of The Great Depression Recipes for Tenacity and Grit Made Easy

Pork Chops with Applesauce

Ingredients:

- 4 pork chops
- Salt, pepper, and preferred seasonings
- 2 tablespoons oil
- 2 cups applesauce

Instructions:

1. Season pork chops with salt, pepper, and preferred spices.

2. In a skillet, heat oil over mediumhigh heat and brown the pork chops on both sides.

3. Transfer pork chops to a baking dish and bake at 375°F for 2025 minutes, until fully cooked.

4. Serve the pork chops with applesauce on the side.

Simplified Cooking From The 1930s With Pictures: The Era Of The Great Depression Recipes for Tenacity and Grit Made Easy

Simplified Cooking From The 1930s With Pictures: The Era Of The Great Depression Recipes for Tenacity and Grit Made Easy

Veal Parmesan

Prep Time: 20 minutes Cook Time: 30 minutes
Servings: 4

Calories: 480 Fat: 24g Carbs: 12g Fiber: 2g
Sugar: 6g Protein: 45g

Ingredients:
- 4 veal cutlets
- 1 cup breadcrumbs
- 1 cup grated Parmesan cheese
- 2 cups marinara sauce
- 1 cup shredded mozzarella
- Olive oil
- Salt and pepper

Instructions:
1. Preheat oven to 375°F (190°C).
2. Season veal with salt and pepper, coat in breadcrumbs and Parmesan.
3. Heat oil in a skillet, brown veal cutlets.
4. Place cutlets in a baking dish, top with marinara and mozzarella.

5. Bake for 20 minutes until cheese is melted and bubbly.

Simplified Cooking From The 1930s With Pictures: The Era Of The Great Depression Recipes for Tenacity and Grit Made Easy

Simplified Cooking From The 1930s With Pictures: The Era Of The Great Depression Recipes for Tenacity and Grit Made Easy

Beef Wellington

Prep Time: 45 minutes Cook Time: 45 minutes
Servings: 6

Calories: 650 Fat: 40g   Carbs: 30g   Fiber: 4g
Sugar: 6g   Protein: 45g

Ingredients:
- Beef tenderloin
- Puff pastry
- Pâté
- Mushrooms
- Shallots
- Egg wash
- Salt and pepper

Instructions:
1. Sear the beef, then cool.
2. Spread pâté over the beef.
3. Cook mushrooms and shallots, cool, then wrap around the beef.
4. Wrap beef in puff pastry, brush with egg wash.

5. Bake until pastry is golden brown.

Simplified Cooking From The 1930s With Pictures: The Era Of The Great Depression Recipes for Tenacity and Grit Made Easy

Simplified Cooking From The 1930s With Pictures: The Era Of The Great Depression Recipes for Tenacity and Grit Made Easy

Oxtail Soup

Prep Time: 30 minutes Cook Time: 3 hours

Servings: 8

Calories: 280 Fat: 10g Carbs: 20g Fiber: 3g

Sugar: 8g Protein: 25g

Ingredients:

- Oxtails
- Onions, carrots, celery
- Beef broth
- Tomatoes
- Bay leaves
- Thyme
- Salt and pepper

Instructions:

1. Brown oxtails in a pot, remove.

2. Sauté vegetables, add oxtails, broth, tomatoes, and herbs.

3. Simmer for 3 hours until meat is tender.

4. Remove oxtails, shred meat, and return to the soup.

Simplified Cooking From The 1930s With Pictures: The Era Of The Great Depression Recipes for Tenacity and Grit Made Easy

CONCLUSION

In a world marked by tumultuous changes and economic instability, the 1930s stands as a pivotal decade that redefined many aspects of society. The era witnessed a transition from extravagance to resourcefulness, from opulence to necessity, leading to a shift in the way people approached cooking and food. "Simplified Cooking from the 1930s" doesn't just capture a collection of recipes; it encapsulates a historical narrative, reflecting the resilience, innovation, and adaptability of a generation in the face of adversity.

This cookbook, with its collection of recipes, evokes the spirit of an era where every ingredient was cherished, and every meal was an act of creativity and ingenuity. The Great Depression prompted a reevaluation of food choices, pushing individuals to maximize limited resources without compromising on flavor and nutrition. Through these recipes, one can grasp the ingenious ways in which cooks of that time transformed simple, readily available ingredients into delectable and nourishing dishes.

Each page of "Simplified Cooking from the 1930s" transports the reader into a world where thriftiness was an art form, and culinary skills were honed out of necessity. The inclusion of vivid pictures serves as a window to this era, depicting not just the dishes but the culture, lifestyle, and ambiance of the 1930s kitchen. These images capture the essence of a period marked by frugality yet imbued with a sense of communal warmth and resilience.

One of the most remarkable aspects of this cookbook is its ability to transcend time. The recipes included, often born out of scarcity, retain their relevance in today's culinary landscape. The innovative use of simple, inexpensive ingredients and efficient cooking techniques are a testament to the timelessness of good, practical cooking. The lessons from this cookbook are not just about recipes but about a mindset—a mindset that encourages resourcefulness, adaptability, and a deep appreciation for the food we consume.

Beyond its culinary offerings, "Simplified Cooking from the 1930s" provides a historical and cultural narrative. It's a gateway into understanding the struggles, triumphs, and creativity of a generation navigating hardships. The cookbook's narrative subtly weaves in societal shifts, economic challenges, and the resilient human spirit that strived to create joy and sustenance amid challenging times.

Moreover, the cookbook serves as a bridge between generations. It enables younger audiences to appreciate the fortitude and inventiveness of their predecessors while providing a sense of nostalgia for those who lived through that time. The visual elements, in particular, render the past vibrant and relatable, appealing to a wide audience seeking not only recipes but a deeper connection with history and the evolution of culinary traditions.

In conclusion, "Simplified Cooking from the 1930s" isn't just a collection of recipes; it's a historical artifact, a cultural compass, and a guide to mindful, practical cooking. It stands as a tribute to the resilience of a generation and the enduring value of resourcefulness. With its rich narrative and imagery, this cookbook invites us to embrace the past, learn from its lessons, and celebrate the remarkable ability of the human spirit to create, adapt, and find joy even in the most challenging times. It's a testament to the saying that through adversity, great innovations and treasures can emerge, even in the kitchen.

Printed in the USA
CPSIA information can be obtained
at www.ICGtesting.com
LVHW022244311024
795407LV00008B/198